I0158987

# A

*is for*

# Answer

# Magick

## Kitchen Table Magick Series

*by*
G. Alan Joel

## Esoteric School of Shamanism & Magic

Copyright © 2022 G. Alan Joel
Esoteric School of Shamanism and Magic, Inc.
All rights reserved.
ISBN: 0-9889112-5-6
ISBN-13: 978-0-9889112-5-3

All rights reserved. No part of this work may be reproduced or utilized in any form or by any means, electronic or mechanical, including photocopying, recording, or by any information storage and retrieval system, without the prior written permission of the author.

Email: *alan@shamanschool.com*
Website: *www.shamanschool.com*

Publisher: Esoteric School of Shamanism and Magic, Inc.

**Disclaimer and Legal Notice:**
The Esoteric School of Shamanism and Magic has made every effort to ensure, at the time of this writing, that the information contained in this book is as accurate as possible. The publisher and author make no warranties or representation with respect to the completeness, fitness, accuracy, applicability, or appropriateness of this book's contents. This book's information is provided strictly for entertainment and educational purposes. Should you choose to use or apply the ideas provided in this book, you take full responsibility for your own actions. The publisher and author provide no guarantee that your life will improve in any way should you choose to use the information presented in this book. The ability of the information provided in this book to provide self-help and life improvement to the reader is entirely dependent upon the reader. The reader's ability to gain positive results from the information presented in this book is entirely dependent on the amount of time the reader devotes to the application of the material in this book, the willingness of the reader to dedicate time and effort to learning the materials presented in this book, as well as the reader's own belief system, which may help or hinder the reader's ability to benefit from this book's materials. Since each reader differs according to willingness and openness to the information available in this book, the author and publisher cannot guarantee success or improvement for every individual reader. Neither the publisher nor the author assumes responsibility for the reader's actions, or whether the information is used for negative or positive purposes. The information contained in this book is drawn from tribal traditions—both modern and ancient—as well as the author's 30 plus years' experience researching and teaching this material to students. The information in this book is presented as interpreted by the author, and, as such, may or may not be entirely accurate. In no way should the information presented in this book be a substitute for advice from health or mental health professionals.

The author and publisher are not liable—or in any way responsible—for actions that the reader may or may not take as a result of reading the information contained in this book. The reader assumes full responsibility for his or her own actions and choices with regard to how he or she chooses to use the information in this book. The reader is strongly encouraged to choose to use the information provided in this book responsibly.

[this page intentionally left blank]

## *Answer Magick Blessing*

Child of Wonder
Child of Flame
Nourish My Spirit and
Protect My Aim.

Answers, answers, where art thou?
I seek Universal guidance, and I need it now!
Angels abound in the Heavens above
Yet walk with us, too, on their journey of love.

Knowledge and guidance are mine to be had
If I but ask, rather than be frustrated or sad.
The Prime Directive a secret to almost all
Means higher beings may not interfered, lest from the higher
they fall!

With these rituals will I learn and perform
I build relationships with beings with higher form.
I stand ready and with an open heart to receive your light
As I know you provide such guidance with love and delight!

With faith and joy on this spiritual path I stride
Awaiting your miracles arriving on a magickal tide.

In advance I thank you for your guidance and lessons
My appreciation for your help is ever present!

Thus, my will, so mote it be!

# Free Gift

To thank you for purchasing this book, I'd like to give you a

100% FREE GIFT

Learn more about your free magickal gift.

## *Access Your Free Gift at*
## *www.shamanschool.com*

*Find a complete list of magickal resources on https://amzn.to/3swxvPo. These resources are constantly updated so check back often!*

[this page intentionally left blank]

# Kitchen Table Answer Magick
# Table of Contents

[this page intentionally left blank]

# *Introduction to Kitchen Table Answer Magick*

*"We're asking you to trust in the Well-being. In optimism there is magic."*
*~Abraham*

## A Note About This Introduction

This book is one of a series of books in the Kitchen Table Magick series. Each book in the series addresses a specific area of magick (love, money, psychic development, etc.), and is written in a simple "recipe" format for people who want to use magick in their lives immediately. The Kitchen Table Magick series is akin to a Julia Childs recipe book, only these books contain magickal recipes for people to cook up some miraculous and magickal manifestations in their lives.

Because this series was designed so that each person could pick and choose to read just the books that pertain to their current life situation, each book is meant to be readable as a stand-alone book. To introduce the new reader to the series, this introduction to the series is repeated at the beginning of each book. If you have already read one or more books in this series, please feel free to jump ahead to the recipes that interest you. At the same time, some people feel that reviewing the introduction, as well as the "Rules and Tips," is helpful before diving in. In magickal circles, your will is the guideline so choose whichever route best suits you... the Universe and magickal beings will follow!

## What is Magick?

Many people have multiple different ideas about what magick is or can be. For the sake of clarity, here is what we know about magick after more than 35 years of study and practice. Magick is a precision science! It is also:

- The science of deliberate creation.
- The science of effective prayer.
- The science of manifesting Higher Will (substitute whatever Higher Force is most familiar to you) on the energetic and material planes.
- The science of heightened awareness, selective perception, and dynamic, harmonious relationships.
- The study of intention (as per Aleister Crowley, one of the greatest magickal practitioners in history).
- The system of creation, not coercion. Note: The word manipulation is often used in conjunction with magick, but manipulation simply means the use of the hands. It should be an "OK" word without a lot of charge, but currently it is used mostly to mean coercion. Look it up!
- The principle that every intentional act is a magickal act! Magic gives us the ability to communicate with beings on all levels, and allows us to understand, through direct experience, the actual workings of the Universe.
- The traditional path of spiritual growth.
- Not extraordinary knowledge. It is the "normal" way of life. We've just lost access to it. When you have this kind of knowledge in your understanding, you have the ability to resolve spiritual questions that otherwise become catechism. From a magickal point of view, catechism is not acceptable, since a practitioner must experience and verify everything for him or herself. It

avoids the trap of dogma. In past times, having a magickal foundation was essential so that we could talk directly to higher beings in the Universal hierarchy.

- Necessary to effective religious practice.

There is some confusion as to how to spell the word "magick." There are three different commonly used spellings: magick, magic, and majick. Eliphas Levi first used the form "magick" to differentiate religious or ceremonial from stage magick. All forms of spelling are acceptable in what this author teaches.

*"I love Kitchen Table Magick! It's the best mix of both mystical and down-to-earth magick I have ever encountered. The fact that I can use items from my pantry is so handy and fun! It literally is about cooking up magic at my kitchen table, and having love show up in the least expected places!"*
*~Wendy J., Skokie, IL*

## Is Magick Real?

Yes. Magick is very real and has existed as a precise science for thousands of years. Whether you use the word magick or another name, this spiritual practice is very real. Every single person can learn to do magick. We are ALL born with the talents and abilities that empower us to do magick. The only reason that magick seems so, well, magickal is that this society no longer teaches the art and science of magick. In the distant past, magickal study was just as important as math, science, or the arts. In fact, magick was and still is the birthright of EVERY planetary citizen.

Can you learn to do the kind of magick portrayed in the movies? Yes... and no. The movies are great at giving you a taste of what you can do with magick, but they are not very accurate. In the Harry Potter movies, for instance, the characters use their Wands for every magickal operation. In reality, you can only use the Wand to handle Air energies. Your Wand would actually explode or catch fire if you tried

to use it to throw Firebolts and Fireballs as the characters do in the movie.

So, what can you actually do with magick? Quite a lot. Here is a short list to get you started:

- Balance your energies for healing and manifestation
- Change old beliefs
- Defend yourself against physical and psychic attack
- Heal yourself and others
- Find hidden information and see possible futures (and change the future if you do not like the probable futures you divine)
- Psychically communicate with other beings
- Create sacred space
- Find lost people and objects
- Manifest what you want and need in life

At the very basis of magick is the understanding of the four elements: Air, Fire, Water, and Earth. Called elemental magick, these foundational elements are real. Air, Fire, Water, and Earth are part of our natural everyday environment. What makes them magickal is the understanding of how they operate not just on the physical level, but also at the levels of Mind and Spirit.

For instance, while on the physical level, Air is just the stuff we breathe. On the magickal levels Air is the conduit of psychic communication, enlightenment, understanding, dreaming, and more. If you want more of these things in your life, then you need more magickal Air. How do you get more magickal Air? Wear more Air colors, including white for communication and sky blue for enlightenment and understanding. To take this one step further, you could also use various magickal techniques to take on more Air to make your body lighter. Take on enough Air and you'll be able to levitate.

By just extending your understanding and use of the basic ingredients of nature, you are doing magick! Seen in this light, magick isn't all smoke and mirrors, nor is it the result of Hollywood special effects. Magic is the result of truly understanding and working with the very elements that are all around you.

One final note: Many masters, including Wayne Dyer, have said, "You'll see it when you believe it." The same is true for magick. In other words, the suspension of disbelief and the willingness not to exercise contempt prior to investigation are requirements for magick to be "real." Magick is all around us, and always is, but our ability to perceive and use the forces of magick depends on our willingness to be open. No one else can show it to you, only your direct experience and observation can "prove" or demonstrate to you that magick is real.

[this page intentionally left blank]

## *What is Kitchen Table Magick?*

Kitchen Table Magick is exactly what it sounds like—a series of simple recipes that you can literally "cook up" at your kitchen table using household ingredients from your own pantry and cupboard.

The Kitchen Table Magic books have been created for ordinary people who want to mix up a little magick in their lives without all the fancy rituals, but simply with everyday ingredients that can be found in the kitchen pantry, bathroom medicine cabinet, or even stuffed in the back of the junk drawer.

The goal of these books is to allow anyone with the desire to learn this craft to mix up magick literally at the kitchen table using simple recipes. What goes into a simple recipe?

- Everyday items as ingredients
- Easy to follow instructions that don't require years of training
- Procedures that take less than two hours from start to finish
- Built-in expertise that allows the magick to do the heavy lifting
- Some friendly advice on how you can help your magickal recipe provide the best results
- Oh, and a few little rules and guidelines about magickal practice in this specific arena that will keep you safe and sound, magickally speaking, when you use these recipes

**Kitchen Table Magick Equals:**
Quick – Effective – Safe – Everyday Use – Ordinary
Affordable Ingredients

## Why Use Kitchen Table Magic?

- Everyone can do magick.
- Magick should be simple, effective, and start working right away, else it is not magick.
- Not everyone has the time or resources to enroll in a school.
- People ask us for magickal help in hundreds of emails everyday... Kitchen Table Magick is designed to help these very people.
- Of the many areas of life, most people only seem to need help in one or two areas, so you need only buy those Kitchen Table Magick books that apply to your needs.
- Magic is for the masses, and should be accessible, affordable, and simple to do. This is what our teacher taught us, and this is the legacy we are paying forward as well.
- While there are many more advanced forms of magick, these books are an introduction to that world so that you can dabble, experiment, try things out, see the result, adjust and amend, and generally have fun... just as you would cooking a meal in your kitchen.
- This book is not for the major foodie, but is perfect for the person who needs magickal help right here, right now!

## Who Should Use These Recipes?

- You and anyone you know who would like a little more magick and a little less ordinary reality in their lives.
- Anyone who needs help RIGHT now and doesn't have time to fly to India or Sedona to sit at the feet of a guru.

Anyone who does not have access to anything but a computer for help and guidance.
- Anyone who wants to do magick and then forget it (all while quietly watching the magick "do its thing").
- Anyone who wants affordable, down to earth magick they can do with regular ingredients in the comfort of home.

## When to Use Kitchen Table Magic: Anytime...
- You need help.
- You don't want to do all the heavy lifting (leave that to the Angels, Spirit Guides, Animal Totems, and so forth).
- You seem stuck in a rut or corner with no way out.
- You've been struggling with a problem for a long time and need a resolution.
- You don't know what to do but you need to do SOMETHING.
- You'd like to learn how to practice the craft.
- You want to live a more magickal life and stop dealing with ordinary hassles all the time.

## How Do We Know These Recipes Work?
- We teach a slew of these recipes in one-day workshops all over the country, via teleconference, and via videoconference. We also email them to people as part of our school's service work, or post them on our blogs and articles library.
- We have used them for over 35 years and still do, every single day – literally tested out at our own kitchen tables for over 35 years (and at thousands of kitchen tables around the world) for a quarter century or more.
- We receive all kinds of stories and testimonials from happy successful students.

# *Kitchen Table Answer Magick at Work...*

Read the following example to discover how Answer Magick works in real life...

## *The Silliest and Most Perfect Answer for a Workaholic*

*"Stuck" is the perfect word to describe my position in life when I once again decided to turn to magick for some help and, hopefully, some useful answers. I say that I turned to magick "again" because I had once been a faithful and dedicated practitioner of the craft for many years, back in my youth. I had found solace, answers, peace, and many useful rituals I could apply to life situations. But somehow, as time went by my focus changed to my career, family (both immediate and extended family), saving for retirement, paying for college... in short, all the usual concerns that take up one's attention in their 30's and 40's. With all of these issues vying for my*

attention, even the simple parts of my magickal practice, such as meditation and the daily greetings to my totems and Spirit Guides, faded away.

But during my mid 40's, I began to feel that something was amiss or awry or just plain "out of whack" in my life. When I looked at the different parts of my life, nothing stood out. My career was on a great path, and I had quickly moved up the management ladder in the last decade. All of my children were in college or had graduated college, and were thriving as they spread their wings. My wife and I had a solid relationship, though both of us worked long hours to keep our careers on track. Nevertheless, we managed to carve out several vacations per year. Everything in my life seemed to be on track, and yet I felt a loss somewhere.

I couldn't figure out why I felt so stuck. In typical Universal fashion, I happened to receive an email from the Esoteric School of Shamanism and Magic, a school where I had learned much of my magickal knowledge. The email announced the beginning of a new self-study course. I was immediately drawn to sign up for the course. It almost felt as if the Universe was pushing me to do so.

## Hello? Universe, Can You Hear Me Now?

The focus of the course was on different ways we could communicate with the Universe to gain answers, guidance, and help from the higher. How perfect! I needed guidance from the higher as to why my life looked perfect from the outside, but I still felt *somehow that something was missing.*

*After so many years of not practicing magick, doing many of the familiar rituals and greetings to Universal beings felt like coming home. I once again practiced using the Water Bowl to communicate with the Universe and ask for guidance. I joyfully greeted the beings of the four directions plus Sky and Earth with the Navajo Beauty Way. I put down roots into Mother Earth and asked for her guidance.*

*I kept getting the same answer, one that completely had me confused and flummoxed. The answer was simply this: "Play more, be playful, work is play and play is work." Say what? When I examined my life, I felt as though I had plenty of opportunities to play. I played squash a few times a week with a buddy from work, I went on a couple of vacations a year with the family, and my wife and I loved to do outdoor activities together (hiking, biking, skiing, and even triathlons).*

*What was the Universe trying to tell me? How else could I add more play into my life when I could barely squeeze my current "play" activities into my schedule before and after work? And how in the world could I make work play when I was one of the top three executives at the firm? Did the Universe expect me to start doing cartwheels down the hall? Work meant high pay, high pressure, high performance, and high achievement. How was I supposed to fit play into that?*

## The Microcosm Exercise

During one of the online chats for the magick course I was taking with the Esoteric School, I asked the teacher for help. He suggested that I use the "microcosm exercise," which allowed me to take the theme the Universe was communicating to me about play, playfulness, and interchanging work and play.

With this exercise, I was to take the basic concept the Universe had communicated to me—play or playfulness—and experiment with this theme in areas of my life where the results of my experimentation did not have a high impact. This magickal exercise is based on the law of "as above, so below." As I learned to "play" in a low-pressure area of my life ("as above") I would begin to see how I could use the same concepts other areas of my life, such as work and being a solid provider for my family ("so below").

Being a confirmed workaholic for years, I really had no idea how to go about being playful in any area of my life. So, I hired an angel to show me at least one area of my life where I could practice being playful without jeopardizing my job, family, or relationships. The angel sent me a dream that very night. The dream was filled with images of my childhood, when I ran with a group of other boys. Together we would pull harmless pranks on each other, always trying to outdo one another. One time I spray-painted my friend's family dog with our high school's colors, much to the amusement of the other boys. Another of our gang pranked me my creating a faux report card showing that I was failing all of my classes. Luckily, he kept my real report card, or else I would have been grounded for months.

Our pranks were always fairly harmless and easily set to rights. But the key factor in all of the pranks was fun and playfulness. We used our ingenuity to see who could "out prank" the other. No matter who was the recipient of the prank, we all had huge amounts of fun. Even in daily conversations we would pull pranks, saying "No" when we meant "Yes," just so we could see the shocked expression on the person's face.

### Pranking and Playfulness in Adult Life

The dream showed me various places in my life where I could once again use the playful side of my nature to introduce some fun and lightheartedness into an otherwise packed schedule of high pressure and high achievement. Of course, as an adult, spray painting the family dog didn't seem to be as much fun as it had been in high school. So, I had to come up with more inventive measures. Many of my new playful acts were completely silly and some of them were truly pranks. Some of the examples included:

- Writing my wife notes in Pig Latin
- Painting my name on the remote control with my wife's lipstick
- Emailing my children that we would be taking our winter vacation in Alaska this year (complete with an attached e-brochure on ice fishing and

dog sledding)
- *Telling my squash partner that I could no longer participate in our twice-weekly games because I had decided to join a meditation group that met every single night after work*
- *Informing my wife that I had agreed to take in four foster children instead of the single foster child we had agreed upon*

*Of course, with all of these pranks I never let the recipient's shock last for more than a few moments. But the joy in planning and executing at least one prank per day truly was fun. In fact, if I pulled a prank in the morning, I would find myself laughing about it all day, especially if the recipient texted me about it or even pranked me back that same day!*

## Playfulness at Work

*While pulling pranks on my boss was definitely out of the question, I did find myself joking with the clerks and assistants at work with great enjoyment. I also found ways to get my work done, yet also add bits of harmless humor into the emails and other more casual forms of communication at work. The best prank yet was when I surprised my entire team (with permission from my boss) by renting a party bus and taking everyone out for Mexican food and margaritas at a local restaurant--this was for a job well done and the completion of a major project. While renting a party bus may not seem like much, in the serious atmosphere of the corporation where I worked, there* wasn't much in the way of celebration. The party bus lifted everyone's mood and playfulness was definitely in the air.

### *After 40 Days*

The "Microcosm Exercise" works best when done 40 days in a row. This meant that I had to find a new way to be playful for 40 days in a row. If I missed a day, I had to start over at Day One. I had to restart this exercise several times, so I ended doing it for about two-and-a-half months. Despite having to start this exercise over a few times, I found that I became fairly skilled at being playful, in small ways and large. More importantly, I had re-established contact with the Universe, my Spirit guides, my animal totems, and scores of angels who were eager to help me with any and every prank and playful act!

Overall, I felt more light-hearted about life, and even my wife commented that I acted more like the man she married many years before. My children, who had rarely seen me be playful, were delighted by the change, and began coming up with their own pranks to play on me. I am most grateful to have reconnected to the Universe. The Microcosm Exercise was wonderful, and this exercise also gave me a chance to receive daily guidance and answers from higher beings. I now find that when I allow the higher beings to do the heavy lifting, I no longer feel the need to be the super achiever in a high-pressure environment. With an entire gaggle of Universal beings at my side, there isn't any need to feel pressured. I

*know that the items that need to be completed will get done, and the rest is just play. Indeed, work is now play and play is now work!*
*~Mike J., Los Angeles, CA*

## *A Few Rules and Tips About Kitchen Table Magick*

As with any game, the game of life has its own set of rules. Specifically, the spiritual side of life has rules. Play by those rules and you will stay safe and easily attract what you want into your life. Break those rules and all types of unwanted consequences happen.

These "spiritual rules" are ones that have been observed, both in personal spiritual practice and spiritual practice with various associated groups and teachers. These rules universally govern any spiritual practice, and appear to be in effect whether you know them or not. Unlike ethics and morals, which change with culture and time, these spiritual rules appear to have remained the same throughout time, unchanging, like physical and scientific rules.

The rules in the following section are adapted from *Rules of the Road*, as created by George Dew, co-founder of the Church of Seven Arrows. There are two major rules, which are common to most spiritual practices, along with some minor rules that are specific to our form of magickal practice.

## Two Major Rules

These two rules will probably sound familiar, as they appear in most major religions and spiritual practices, most probably because they are common-sense and apply not just to spiritual practice, but to life as well.

### *First Rule: Golden Rule or Law of Karma*

This first rule is literally a "golden oldie":

*What you do to the environment or to other beings in the environment brings similar effects back to you in your life.*

Often recognized as the Golden Rule or the Law of Karma, this rule tops the list because it reminds all spiritual practitioners of potential unwanted "rebound" or side effects. As your spiritual power, focus, and abilities grow, this rule will have an ever-greater impact on your life unless you exercise caution. The Universe responds more strongly and powerfully to those with focus, power, and ability.

***Note***: As humanity moves further in the Aquarian Age, many spiritual practitioners have seen more effects from this rule occur faster. In the past, effects of this rule that often took lifetimes to manifest now occur in minutes, days, weeks, or months. In this particular time in Earth's history, karma seems to operate under a "pay as you go" system. Simply stated, expect the effects of the Law of Karma to occur quickly.

### *Second Rule: The Judgment of "Good and Bad" According to the Universe*

This second rule adds clarity and detail to the first rule described previously:

*If you are unsure whether your acts are "good or bad"--*

*that is, whether those acts are in keeping with universal laws on this planet—the Universe will reflect its judgment back to you quickly, according to the "pay as you go" Law of Karma.*

This law holds as true for individuals as it does for entire communities, states, nations, or other organized groups. If you are still unsure of the feedback you receive from the Universe, check areas such as your level of health, the soundness of social relationships, your prosperity or lack of, sufficiency of various needs in life, and even your "luck" with appliances and machines. If your luck appears to be consistently poor, then you are probably acting contrary to universal governing laws, regardless of your intentions. The Universe cares about what you do more than what you intend.

### *Additional Detailed Rules*
The following rules offer more detailed standards by which to measure your acts or the acts of others to determine whether these acts are in accordance with universal laws.

- Do nothing that will harm another being unless you are willing to suffer similar or greater harm. What the Universe considers "harm" may be different than what you consider harm.
- Do not bind another being unless you are willing to be similarly bound. An example of binding someone is doing acts in attempt to coerce a specific other person to love you. There is no problem with attracting your soul mate into your life, but doing acts that attempt to coerce a specific other person to love you is a type of binding.
- Never use your spiritual abilities in vain, to show off, or to boost your pride. Using your spiritual abilities from a place of pride usually causes the Universe to bring instant backlash into your life.
- If you choose to charge money or barter for using your spiritual abilities in the service of others, avoid

charging extremely high prices. Charge prices for using methods comparable to other professionals, such as an attorney or accountant.

- Never use any spiritual word, chant, litany, or similar "device" unless you are confident in your understanding of its methods, intents, and effects.
- When undertaking a major spiritual operation—one that will require significant effort or attempts to create a major effect in the world—use divination to determine whether you can safely benefit from such an operation, and to discover the obstacles you must overcome. Divination methods such as pendulum readings, channeling, meditation, and question circles (to name a few) can reveal hidden factors of which you may be unaware.
- In any spiritual endeavor, take your time, think it through, and do it right!

The good news is that you can still perform answer magick rituals. The ones we teach in this book won't get you in trouble with the Universe, yet will still allow you to attract the answers that you seek into your life. While you can't lobby the Universe for a specific answer, you can ask the Universe for guidance on anything and everything, and the Universe will always answer your call!

# The Ingredients of Answer Magick

*"The universe never says no to your thought*
*about yourself. It only grows it."*
*~ Neale Donald Walsch*

People often write us asking for help in receiving answers from the Universe. These people have often tried multiple methods of divination (pendulum dowsing, Tarot readings, and more), or sought help from people who channel specific Spirits. Even these people always receive some kind of answer from the people from whom they sought help, the answers just didn't seem quite "right."

Either the answers felt generic and didn't really apply to the person's specific situation, or the answers were specific but the reasoning behind the answer did not sit well with the person seeking guidance. These people are perfectly correct when they tell us that the answers they have received so far just didn't feel "on" or "right" or "personal" or "justified." Whatever the adjectives used to describe the person's frustration, these people are completely correct in their feelings about the guidance they had so far received. Feelings and emotions, after all, are the language of Spirit, so when someone "feels" that the guidance being given is a little "off," they are receiving a message from their Spirit telling them that the guidance isn't quite right.

## What's Up with Answers That Feel "Off"?

What does it mean if you seek answers from a medium who channels, a person who offers Tarot readings, or any other source of Universal guidance, and you just don't feel comfortable with those answers? When you get these "gut feelings" about the answers you receive, follow your gut. Your innate sense of Spirit guidance will never lead you astray. When you feel that the answers you receive are not correct, listen to your Spirit voice... go with your gut.

If you have received accurate information from these sources in the past, but now feel that the guidance being offered is no longer accurate, you are bound to wonder what has changed? Why has a previously reliable source suddenly become incorrect in the answers or guidance it offers? Has that source of spiritual guidance suddenly lost all perspective?

This is a smart and savvy question. The answer is, "Probably not." It is not unusual for a previously reliable source of spiritual guidance to suddenly be unable to offer you the guidance you seek. Why does this happen? This happens for the simple reason that both the Universe and your own inner Spirit are guiding you to the realization that you have evolved far enough on your spiritual journey in this lifetime that you are now better served by having a direct link to the Universe. Early in your spiritual journey, it is more difficult to achieve direct contact with the Universe. It is even more difficult to establish a working relationship with the higher beings in the Universal hierarchy, much less have a constant "back and forth" conversation about any and all forms of guidance you might need in your life.

When you have journeyed far enough on your spiritual path, though, you will suddenly find that you can no longer easily receive accurate guidance from outside sources. The time has come for you to establish contact with the Universe, and receive direct guidance from the various beings in the Universal hierarchy. This hierarchy includes angels, elementals (of Air, Fire, Water, and Earth), along with the Winds of the four Directions, Sky Father, Earth Mother, and many more beings too numerous to name here. Suffice to say there are many beings in the Universal Hierarchy, each with its own specialty and area of responsibility. Once you have established a connection with the Universe using the first few exercises offered in this book, you will then be able to identify and work with specific beings in the Hierarchy, as well as the Universe in general.

## The Main Ingredient of Answer Magick

As you may have already realized through your own experience, one of the main ingredients of Answer Magick is a direct connection to the Universe. Not only is this necessary for each person at a certain point in his or her spiritual journey, but to receive answers that are personal and customized specifically for your current life situation requires having multiple conversations with the Universe. For instance, you may ask the Universe a question, and the Universe delivers the answer.

Early on in your conversations with the Universe, you may misinterpret the answer, be confused by the answer, or simply miss the answer altogether. What then? No worries. Thank the Universe for sending the answer (always thank the Universe and beings in the Universal hierarchy before, during, and after a request for help or answers). Then request that the Universe send the answer again, this time in a way that you can clearly understand. Ask for clarification. Ask for the answer to be more obvious. Simply keep asking the Universe for clarification of the answer you seek, day after day, until the answer becomes so obvious you will literally trip over it.

Direct contact with the Universe is a "must" at a certain point in your spiritual evolution. This is true for anyone evolving spiritually, but also true for many people in the Aquarian Age. During the previous Piscean Age, people received many of the answers they needed from gurus and people who channeled the essence of various spiritual beings, and other similar sources. But in the Aquarian Age, gurus are proving less useful, and a direct personal connection with the Universe is more likely to yield the answers you seek.

Beyond direct contact with the Universe, though, there is also a need to establish a strong, solid, and trusting relationship with the Universe. Unlike a computer, the Universe is a real, live, animated, and spiritual being. So, working with the Universe means that you must begin to converse with the Universe just as you might strike up a conversation with a total stranger, only to find that the relationship deepens and becomes a source of mutual feedback and enjoyment. As with any stranger you meet, at first you will start with small talk when conversing with the Universe. Ask for small answers and guidance, and practice looking for the answers. If you don't understand the answer, ask again and again until the answer becomes crystal clear. This repeated asking for and receiving of answers is the beginning of a long and beautiful relationship with the Universe. So long as you treat with the Universe with respect, just as you would your best friend, plus follow the Rules of the Road, the Universe can and will become the ultimate source of guidance and answers in your life.

Appreciation, gratitude, thanks, and respect are all that the Universe requires in return for the limitless and wise guidance it can provide to you. When you request help from the Universe, always thank the Universe directly after the request and before the answer or guidance appears in your life. When you receive the answer, sincerely thank the Universe again (even if you don't understand the answer and must ask for clarification). The same kind of appreciation is the spiritual coin of payment when you begin working with specific beings in the Universal hierarchy, including angels, elemental beings, the Winds, weather working Spirits, planetary guardians, and more.

# Working with Specific Universal Beings

As you work your way through the magickal rites and rituals in this book, you may find that certain spiritual beings begin appearing in your life to provide answers. These specific beings may include animal totems. Spirit guides, Spirits of long-departed ancestors, or even garden gnomes that live on your property.

The beauty of working with specific spiritual beings is that their specialized talents can often provide you with more customized information than the general Universe. For instance, if you want to learn how to enjoy life more and play more (as you did when you were younger), the Hummingbird animal totem may show up in your life. Hummingbirds are joyful creatures who enjoy flitting from one beautiful flower to another, hovering around us at times to radiate their joy and share their essence. For protection, you may find that certain guardians appear in your life. Some may be the Spirits of warriors past while others may be personal Spirit guides who lead you towards safety in your choices and decisions.

No matter what your current need may be for guidance or answers, beginning a dialog with the Universe is the place to start. From there, move from small talk to discussions of greater importance. Once you see that the Universe always delivers, and is never impatient when you repeatedly ask for clarification, the conversation with the Universe will become less formal and more easygoing. At this point, other helpful angels, animal totems, Spirit guides, and beings able to guide you in your specific needs will appear in your life.

To have this kind of the relationship with the Universe and various specific Universal helpers, all you need to do is make contact with the Universe. Open the door and invite the Universe into your life. Without such an invitation the Universe may have all the guidance you seek but cannot give it to you. This is because the Prime Directive is one the Universal Laws that governs planet Earth. Universal and spiritual beings may not interfere in our lives because we have free will. Any interference without an invitation violates our free will (even if our free will gets us in all kinds of trouble).

The first step, then, is to invite the Universe and its various helpers into your life. The second step is to develop a one-on-one relationship with the Universe. Start small. Request help and guidance for lesser issues at first. Once you trust that the Universe answers every request for help, and once the Universe realizes that you always express sincere gratitude and appreciation for the help you have received, your relationship is well on its way to being deep, loyal, and of mutual benefit and enjoyment. At this point you can move on to asking for help on bigger and thornier issues in your life. You may have to ask for clarification many times, and this only deepens your relationship.

Always remember that the Universe is a living Spirit, just as you are a living Spirit. The Universe is alive... it is not a computer that spits out answers on command. So treat the Universe as you would treat any mentor or elder. Offer respect, thanks, and gratitude frequently. At the same time, don't be afraid to ask for the answers and guidance that you need, nor be afraid to ask for clarification as often as possible. The Universe is infinitely patient and knows more about you and your life situations than you do. Learn to trust to the Universe as your relationship progresses, and you will be rewarded richly not just with answers and guidance, but also with a deep, rich, and complex relationship that will be unique in your life.

# *Answer Magick Appetizer Recipes*

## Appetizers: Making Contact with the Universe for Answers

### *The Navajo Beauty Way Exit Ritual*

### *Send a Fireball Message to the Universe*

*"I definitely had my doubts about getting actual useful information from 'unseen Spirits.' After all I was unsure I would be able to tell whether I was hearing my own thoughts or actually receiving information from the Universe. What made me a believer was the fact that the information I got was nothing like I would ever think of."*
*~ Fred W., Hopland, CA*

[this page intentionally left blank]

# *The Navajo Beauty Way Exit Ritual*

*"The key to growth is the introduction of higher dimensions of consciousness into our awareness."*
*~ Lao Tzu*

**Time Required: Fifteen Minutes**

One of the best ways to establish an ongoing relationship with the myriad of higher beings in the Universe is by doing a daily ritual called the Navajo Beauty Way. Although this ritual is currently thought to originate from the Navajo tribe, in reality the three rituals that comprise the Beauty Way have been practiced by various tribes around the globe for centuries. The Beauty Way is a non-denominational set of exercises that was created in very ancient times.

There are three parts to this ritual: Exit Ritual, Day Greetings and Day Endings, and the Walking Litany. In this recipe, you will learn how to use the Exit Ritual to connect to Sky and Earth. Among its many other spiritual benefits, the Exit Ritual a great way to establish a working relationship with higher powers, beings, and natural forces and laws.

29

## Ingredients

- A desire to overcome any embarrassment factor or self-consciousness when doing this ritual in public
- A spirit of being open to communications in whatever form they may come

## Recipe Directions

1. Anytime you go outside or leave an enclosed area such as a building or your car, take a few moments to pause.
2. As you pause, put your focus up into the sky and say aloud, "Sky Above" or "Sky Father." (To start you can mouth the words and say them in your mind if you are self-conscious in public).
3. Keep your awareness up above, while at the same time extending your focus into the earth and say aloud, "And Earth Below" or "And Earth Mother."
4. Last, keep your awareness both above and below, say aloud, "I Greet You".
5. Continue pausing to see what happens. You may have a message from within such as a new realization, a change in attitude or belief or a new awareness or there may be a change in the environment around you such as a sudden breeze or an animal appearing or you could get a particular message you "hear" from Sky Father or Earth Mother giving you guidance or answering a question you have.

## How to Use the Results of Your Recipe

You may notice results in just that moment or it may happen throughout the day. It may change the quality of your day, your awareness, or guidance that appears in unexpected ways. If you feel comfortable doing so, you can also use hand gestures along with this ritual. When addressing Sky Father, raise your arms in an upward facing V and when addressing Earth Mother move your arms down in a downward facing V."

# *Send a Fireball Message to the Universe*

*"We live in times of high stress. Messages that are simple, messages that are inspiring, messages that are life-affirming, are a welcome break from our real lives."*
*~Simon Sinek*

**Time Required: Thirty Minutes**

With the Navajo Beauty Way Exit Ritual, you established contact with higher beings in the Universe. The next step is to deepen your connection with these higher beings by sending a Universe a message. More specifically, you will learn to create a Fireball and program it with a request for information or feedback from the Universe.

Fireballs are formed by shaping one of the four elements (Air, Fire, Water, and Earth) into a ball. Even though these magickal energy forms are called Fireballs, they can be constructed from any of the four elements according

31

to the purpose of the Fireball. You can also use a box shape to hold any one of the four elements, but these are not as stable and will eventually break up even if not disposed of properly. Fireballs are self-cohesive and can exist indefinitely if they are not used or are not properly disposed of. They are often used in self-defense magic since they deliver a stronger effect than a box shape. A Fireball's durability also makes it an excellent energy forms for sending messages to the Universe. There are three methods of constructing Fireballs. The following recipe gives you the easiest and fastest method. The recipe will then give you directions for sending messages to the Universe and Universal helpers.

## Ingredients
- A bright yellow color source (any item that is bright yellow, called Sun Yellow, with no hint of red or orange). This color source can be a vase, a yellow poster board, a sunflower, etc.
- A willingness to be open to responses from the Universe (in whatever form they may take)

## Recipe Directions
This method of making Fireballs is called the Clapping Method. This recipe uses the Sun Yellow Color, which is a safe Fire element color. Sun Yellow boosts Spirit energy, and makes an excellent color for communicating with higher beings in the Universe.

1. Start by standing so that the Sun Yellow energy source (item) is behind you. Feel yourself pulling in the energy from the color source into your shoulders from behind while holding your hand wide apart with palms and finger curved as you would if you were about to clap or catch a ball. Don't think about "how" to pull the energy from the color source, just do it. Your intention will pull the Sun Yellow energy into your body automatically.

2. Continue pulling the energy in from behind through your shoulders and down into your arms and out your hands.

3. Once you feel the energy is flowing strongly into your body, clap your hands together forcefully and stop when your fingertips come together. This compresses the energy flowing from your hands into a ball. Keep your hands cupped as if holding a small ball and do not let your hands or fingers collapse.

4. Next, shape your Fireball and add force to it. Move your hands as if you were shaping and packing a snowball, and then begin to spin the energy ball clockwise.

5. Once the ball is spinning, you can program it with the message that you want to send out to the Universe. If you have a specific higher being with whom you want to communicate, such as a specific angel or Spirit guide, put that being's name inside the Fireball. Simply see the letters of the being's name spelled out in the Fireball. Some people find this process easier to complete with their eyes closed. If you don't have a specific higher being in mind, simply put the word "Universe" in the Fireball.

6. Now program the Fireball with your request or question. The easiest way is to speak your message directly into the Fireball, using your intention to "push" the message into the Fireball. Your Fireball will feel more "charged" or "energized" once your request or question has been firmly lodged inside the Fireball.

7. To send the message, throw the Fireball up and away from you. Since the Fireball has been programmed to

seek either a specific higher being or the Universe in general, the Fireball will automatically find the programmed being.

8.  Feel free to repeat this process once a day for several day (up to 40 days if you wish). Although higher beings and the Universe will definitely receive your first message, sending your message multiple times can demonstrate your dedication and desire to receive feedback, answers, or help from the higher beings.

9.  If you do not use the Fireball to send a message (if you are only practicing creating Fireballs), you must dispose of them properly. With this Sun Yellow Fireball, the safe way to dispose of it is to throw it into a corner in a room or smash it against the ground. Be sure to never aim it at a person or other living thing as the Universe will hold you responsible for any harm that comes to them as a result. In the case of a Sun Yellow Fireball, the person could become hyper or spacey, which could be dangerous (for instance, if the person is driving). This is the method for disposing of Sun Yellow Fireballs, but it is not the proper way to dispose of all Fireballs made of other elements.

## How to Use the Results of Your Recipe

Now that you have sent your message out to the Universe or higher being, look for signs and messages that will provide you with the information or guidance you have asked for. These communications may appear in surprising ways, so be alert for them. You may hear something in a conversation with another person that will open your eyes to a new awareness. Or you may be drawn to a book in a bookstore, come across a website while surfing the internet, or find your answer or Universal feedback in any number of ways. The Universe will use any and all ways to communicate with you until you get the requested help or information you seek. If you don't find the answers you are looking for, you may need to send your message out again and specify that the answer appear in a way that you can more easily understand. The Universe is always happy to clarify and repeat feedback until you get the help or information you seek.

[this page intentionally left blank]

# *Answer Magick Main Course Recipes*

## Creating a Deeper Relationship with the Universe

### *Use a Water Bowl to Create s Spirit Link with the Universe*

### *Rooting to Gain Answers from Mother Earth*

### *Attract Answers by Creating a Microcosm*

*"Whenever I have felt lost, alone, and hopeless, all I have ever had to do is to ask the Universe for help and answers. The answers that I receive always astound me with their accuracy and details. My only job is to ask, and then stay open to the answers! How easy is that?"*
*~ Kim J., El Paso, TX*

[this page intentionally left blank]

# Use a Water Bowl to Create a Spirit Link with the Universe

*"Enlightenment, for a wave in the ocean, is the moment the wave realizes it is water. When we realize we are not separate, but a part of the huge ocean of everything, we become enlightened. We realize this through practice, and we remain awake and aware of this through more practice."*
*~ Thich Nhat Hanh*

**Time Required: Sixty Minutes**

A Water Bowl is a magkical technique that allows you to use your own innate magickal elemental Water to communicate with the Universe or any other Spirit beings on a psychic or Spirit level. As a human being, you possess all four of the magickal elements of Air, Fire, Water, and Earth. As you will learn in this exercise, you can call forth your innate Water element, and use that Water as a communication tool. In this section of the book, you will learn to use your Water element to create a Water Bowl.

The Water Bowl is just one of the many ways that you

can use your magickal Water element as a magickal tool. For instance, you can blast unwanted Spirits with Water element from a magickal Chalice. You can heal many physical illnesses by using water to increase circulation, push unwanted toxins out of the body, or add more magickal Water to your own constitution to increase your psychic abilities. In this exercise you will learn to build and use a Water Bowl as a communication device with the Universe. Water Bowls can also be used for a variety of other magickal operations, such as divination, finding lost objects, calming your emotions, and re-balancing your body for self-healing.

## Ingredients

- A Water Blue color source (any object that is colored Water Blue) that you will use as a reference color to build a Water Bowl. If you have a choice between a darker or lighter blue, choose the lighter blue source as darker Water Blue can bring up strong emotions that will not be useful for this exercise. Your Water Blue source could be anything from a piece of paper to a water glass of the right color.
- Pen and paper for recording the results of your Water Bowl conversation with Universal beings

## Recipe Directions

1. Place your Water Blue color source close by so that you can easily see it and use it as a reference for flowing the right color.

2. Sit in a comfortable position in which you can rest your elbows against your sides just above your hip bones.

3. Extend arms and hands horizontally in front of you with your fingertips interlaced. This forms the "bowl" just above your navel level. The "bowl" should not be any higher or any lower than this. As you read through and perform the following instructions,

simply do instructed acts. Do not think about "how" to do these operations, or allow your mind to question these instructions. Creating a Water Bowl is not a thinking operation. You simply form a Water Bowl by doing the following steps. Excess thinking will simply get in the way, so keep a quiet mind as you create your Water Bowl.

4. Envision or "mock-up" a dry stream bed, ditch, or faucet spout coming from the area of your heart and into or over the bowl.

5. Look at your Water Blue color source. Pull that Water Blue energy from your color source into your body, into your heart, from which the magickal Water element spouts into the bowl formed by your arms and interlaced fingers. Keep the Water pouring out of the spout or stream and into the bowl you have built with your arms and body.

6. Keep flowing this energetic Water until the bowl is full and reaches the edges. When the Water Bowl is full, you will probably feel a coolness or pressure on your arms or fingers.

7. Now that you have a full Water Bowl, the next step is to smooth the surface on the Water before you use the Water to communicate or send messages to the Universe. To smooth the surface of the water, begin absorbing the Water energies in the bowl back into your body, then circulate the Water so it spouts forth from your heart area to create a continuous flow. Most people find that absorbing the magickal Water energies up their arms, and then flowing it to the spout at the heart level is the simplest way to circulate the Water energy in the Water Bowl.

8. As you re-circulate your magickal Water in this

manner, let any stress or turbulent feelings flow into the energetic Water. Continue re-circulating the Water until you have a smooth surface in the bowl. To create a smooth surface in your Water bowl, you may need to keep re-circulating your magickal Water for several minutes.

9. When you have achieved a smooth surface in your Water Bowl, stop re-circulating the Water energy. If energetic Water appears as dark blue or blue-black, then reabsorb all the water energy and stop the procedure. Start the process over from the beginning. This time, choose a lighter Water Blue color source, and as you flow and re-circulate your energetic Water, focus on keeping the color of the Water in the Water Blue light and full of bright energy.

10. Once you have a quiet and smooth surface in your Water Bowl, avoid making sudden movements or dropping the Water Bowl. The Water Bowl is full of your magickal Water, and allowing that Water to slosh over the edges, or dropping the Water Bowl, can create a strong negative emotional effect or cause dehydration. Water Blue represents the emotions (the language of Spirit) as well as the physical water in your body. If you get sloppy with the Water in the Water Bowl, and allow this magickal energy to be lost, it will take weeks or longer to recover both emotionally and physically. As with all magickal operations, "Take your time, think it through, and do it right!"

11. You are now ready to use the Water Bowl for conversing with or sending messages to the Universe or Universal beings. Start by getting very interested in the Universal being with whom you want to communicate. Feel a strong desire to establish a communication link with those beings. If possible,

"see" the Universal being or beings in your Water bowl. While you may not know what these Universal beings look like, simply imagine their images, and see them in your Water Bowl. Your intention will attract those beings with whom you wish the communicate to your Water Bowl, regardless of whether your image of them is accurate. At first, you may find it easier to close your eyes to "see" the images in the Water Bowl with your mind's eye. Some people close their eyes, and then discover that the images from the Water Bowl seem to appear behind their heads. It does not matter where you "see" the images in the Water Bowl, so long as you are able to see the being or beings with whom you wish to communicate.

12. Once you see the image of the Universal being with whom you wish to communicate, you have established a link with that being, and you are ready to begin a dialog. Focus on the image of that Universal being in your Water Bowl and speak normally (as you would to another person). Keep your focus and intent strong, avoiding outside distractions or influences. Greet the Universal being, and then state your request, question, or simply begin a conversation. One you have stated your request, thank the Universal being in advance for their presence as well as their responses to come.

13. The Water Bowl forms a two-way link which allows you to both speak to and listen to the Universal being. Once you have opened the conversation and have stated your need or request, pause to listen for responses. Remember that the Water Bowl forms a Spirit-to-Spirit connection, so you may receive unexpected answers, since Spirit sees the world differently than we do. We are Spirits who tend to see the world through the five senses. The responses you receive may be a voice in your head, images, or even

written words. You will most likely receive an immediate answer, and it is also possible that you will receive answers throughout the day, so be alert to these types of responses.

14. Once the conversation is complete, often signified by the lack further responses from the Universal being, thank the being for their help. You may see the image of the Universal "wink out" or simply disappear from your Water Bowl.

15. The final step is to take down your Water Bowl carefully, so that you don't lose any spiritual or physical Water. To take down your Water Bowl, simply absorb your energetic Water from the bowl back into your body through your palms and arms. When the Water Bowl feels empty, unlock your fingers. Be sure that all of your energetic Water is absorbed before disassemble the bowl. If you don't pull all your water energy back in, you may feel emotionally drained or physically dehydrated later.

## How to Use the Results of Your Recipe

Since Water is the element related to emotions, as well as the language of Spirit, the Water Bowl is a wonderful way to communicate with a variety of Universal beings. You may receive responses directly from the Universal beings in your Water Bowl. Once you have safely disassembled your Water Bowl, record as much of the conversation as you can remember on your pad of paper.

You may also receive messages later in the day, so you may wish to carry pen and paper with you during the day to record further messages. Be aware for any signs and guidance from the Universal beings from the Water Bowl. These may appear as animal totems, snippets of conversation overheard during the day, a sentence from a magazine article... in short, messages may take any number of forms. Keep your senses open for anything out of the ordinary, or anything pertaining to your topic of interest from the Water Bowl. You may be amazed at how much information you receive, both immediately in the Water Bowl, and later as you move through your day. Universal beings are always happy to help. Be sure to express your gratitude and thanks each time you receive a bit of helpful information or guidance. If any messages are unclear, you can do another Water Bowl—or even an entire series of Water Bowls—to ask for clarification. The Universe never tires of being invited into your world to offer help and guidance. If you are confused by any if the responses you receive, don't hesitate to ask for clarification over and over until you gain the clarity you seek!

[this page intentionally left blank]

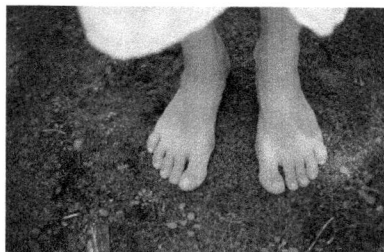

# Rooting to Gain Answers from Mother Earth

*"Our feet are our body's connection to the earth."*
*~ Andrew Weil*

**Time Required: Thirty Minutes**

With the Navajo Beauty Way Exit Ritual, you learned to connect with both Sky Father and Earth Mother (or Sky Above and Earth Below). With the following recipe, you will learn to connect with the Earth, also known as "Mother Earth" or "Grandmother," depending on the magickal ritual you are using, to gain answers. As with the Water Bowl, you can also use your connection with Earth Mother to rebalance your energies and rejuvenate yourself. Earth Mother has a much greater mass, and therefore can take much more of any of your excess energies of all four types: Air, Fire, Water, and Earth. Earth Mother can also provide minerals and nutrients for your body, along with nourishment for your Spirit.

If you frequently travel out-of-body, whether with intent or by accident, learning how to root with the following recipe can help your Spirit stay in your body. Many people travel out-of-body during the night, as they sleep, which can

47

be disconcerting, and can cause a lack of sleep. Rooting nightly before going to sleep can prevent this nightly Spirit travel.

Rooting can also be used to anchor yourself with Mother Earth on a physical level to keep your footing on slippery surfaces or in slippery conditions, or to keep someone from pushing you around. In the directions below you will begin by extending roots from the heels of the feet, but roots can actually be extended from the palms of your hands, the base of your spine or just about any joint in your body.

## Ingredients

- A comfortable place to sit where you can put your bare feet directly in contact with the Earth
- Several minutes of quiet time and space
- Pen and paper for recording the results of your Water Bowl conversation with Universal beings

## Recipe Directions

1. Sit in a comfortable chair (or stand) with your feet touching the ground. Depending on weather conditions and personal preference, you may wish to wear shoes or put your bare feet directly in contact with the Earth to connect with Mother Earth. Sitting indoors and wearing shoes is also fine if the weather or preference does not allow you to directly connect with Mother Earth with bare feet.

2. Once you are comfortably seated or standing, you can begin to send roots into Mother Earth. See and feel yourself extending roots out of your heels, through the flooring, into the sub-floor and foundation and down into the ground. If you are in a building that has several floors, see your roots extending through each floor. Don't waste time using your mind to follow these directions. Simply extend roots into the Earth. Your body and Spirit will know what to do.

3. When your roots reach the Earth, continue extending them through the topsoil, and through each layer of Earth until you get to bedrock.

4. Once you reach bedrock, lock your roots in. Literally dig your roots into the bedrock and curl them into a locked position.

5. Sit in this position, and breathe, flowing any excess energies into the Earth. For example, you can flow excess Fire energies, such as tension or anger through your roots and down into the Earth with each exhalation. Mother Earth is a very receptive being and can easily receive these energies. Excess emotions are Water energies. Excess thoughts are Air energies. Excess rigidity is Earth energy. Mother Earth can accept large amounts of our energies, so don't be afraid to keep flowing excess or unwanted energies through your roots in Mother Earth.

6. Mother Earth can also nourish your body, mind, and Spirit. As you inhale, pull in minerals, fluids and other energies from Mother Earth to nourish your mind, body, and spirit. You can also pull in energies through your roots to rebalance yourself on any level—Spirit, mind, and body.

7. Once you feel complete with your rooting—having rid yourself of excess energies and nourished yourself with energies from the Earth—you must pull your roots back up into your body before you move. See and feel yourself unlocking your roots from the bedrock, pulling them up through the layers of earth, through the topsoil, back through the sub-flooring and flooring and completely back up into your heels. If you move before pulling up your roots, you may feel a popping sensation and your feet will be sore for several days. If you do move before pulling up roots,

flow red orange Fire energy (pain) into a large electric ground like a refrigerator for pain relief.

8. With practice, you can learn to root into Mother Earth quickly for balance or protection. For instance, if you are walking on a slippery surface, you can quickly send roots into the Earth and quickly lock your roots to stabilize yourself. Instead of extending long roots, extend small claw-like roots from each foot. Before you pick up each foot to take the next step, be sure to quickly draw your roots back into your feet. You can also use the same technique if someone is trying to push you around. You can quickly root to lower your center of gravity, and lock your body in one spot.

## How to Use the Results of Your Recipe

Besides helping you to energetically balance yourself, this connection with Earth Mother can be used in situations where you need to pull excess Fire energy but can't access an electrical ground to safely dispose of it. This could be in a situation where there is a noisy or angry crowd that you need to deal with. Earth Mother can also help you protect yourself by giving you an anchor if someone is harassing you physically, mentally or spiritually. If you find yourself in a confrontational situation like this, just quickly begin extending roots and push your heels down for the roots to extend stronger and more quickly. If you have problems with traveling out-of-body when you are asleep, rooting can help you stayed anchored to get a good night's sleep. Just put down your roots through the bed before going to sleep and you'll be able to keep yourself in your body. You can extend roots from your feet, hands, spine, and neck. Just be sure to pull up the roots in the morning before getting out of bed.

Earth Mother can be a stabling and anchoring influence in your life, especially if you use rooting on a regular basis. You will find yourself more balanced on all levels. Excess energies will be less likely to overwhelm you. If you tend to "blow your top" too easily, regular rooting with Earth Mother will decrease your excess Fire energies, and you will find yourself more even-tempered. Rooting will also keep your nourished on all levels, and you will find that, with regular rooting, your energy levels are higher and you feel stronger and have greater endurance.

[this page intentionally left blank]

# *Attract Answers by Creating a Microcosm*

*"Once you make a decision, the universe conspires to make it happen."*
*~Ralph Waldo Emerson*

**Time Required: Sixty Minutes**

This technique allows you to access wisdom from the Universe to help you solve life's problems and make changes in your life. It is particularly useful for issues that seem to have a repetitive pattern in your life. It could be you seem to always have money issues, relationship issues, issues with career or weight or family that you just can't seem to overcome. The Universe can help you see where these issues are coming from, why you keep attracting them, and can't seem to make them stop. The Universal law of "as above, so below" allows you to re-create your life as a microcosm that you can observe and study to find where the difficulties lie.

Then using this information, you will be able to make a small change in the present which leads to a larger change in the future. By making a change within this microcosm, the change also occurs in your real life. For this recipe we will use the example of a person who is always short of money because she impulsively buys things that she doesn't really need, and can't seem to stop. The same recipe directions can be applied to any problem in your life.

## Ingredients

- A willingness to experiment with change
- A relationship established with the Universe and willingness to be open to communications from it
- Some uninterrupted time and an area to sit quietly to hear guidance from the Universe
- A journal or Book of Shadows to write in

## Recipe Directions

1. Sit for several minutes just focusing on the problem and aloud invite the Universe to help you see a theme for your problem. In this example the theme might be "What you don't need."

2. Now again asking for guidance, identify the "theme" of the solution. In this example that might be "Conserve". That means you want to stop using your resources on what you don't need.

3. Decide on an area of your life that is NOT the problem area where you can work on the solution theme. In this example, you want to practice conserving, but not in the area of money since this is the problem and you have not had success with it.

4. Examples of other areas to practice conserving might include:
   - talking when you don't need to

- acting when you don't need to (ie. – taking over projects from others)
- excessive thinking or worrying

5. If you are having trouble identifying other areas, ask for the Universe to help you find one. Chances are that if this is a problem in one area of your life, it exists in other areas too. If you are having difficulty getting the messages and input you need from the Universe, writing about it often is a way to clarify and receive information and inspirations.

6. After you have identified an area to practice conserving that is not related to money, set yourself a goal for practicing. It could start with one time each day. Pick a conversation in which you only say what is absolutely necessary, and conserve your breath.

7. At the end of each day, record your goal and the results you had in a journal or Book of Shadows.

8. Continue this for 40 days (which is the time frame it takes to make any real change in a habitual behavior). At the end of the 40 days, review what you have written in your journal to see what changes have occurred.

## How to Use the Results of Your Recipe

By practicing the law of conservation by talking less, you will find it also transfers to your spending habits. The key to this magickal technique is to work through the problem in a relatively benign way. Once the problem is worked out in this way, it will have worked its way out in your life as well. By creating a microcosm of your life, what works in the goal you set for yourself applies everywhere else in life. And with the guidance and input from the Universe, you will finally be able to identify those stumbling blocks that have alluded you before.

# *Answer Magick Dessert Recipes*

## Desserts: Quick and Practical Answer Recipes

### *Use Dowsing for Practical Answers*

### *Pick a Card, Any Card*

*"One of my favorite things about these magickal 'recipes' is that I can use everyday items to whip up the magick I seek. A book, the verses from a song, a bird flying by—these can all be magickal gifts and words from the Universe. I am literally surrounded by magick everywhere I go."*
*~ Jules T., Duluth, MN*

[this page intentionally left blank]

# Use Dousing for Practical Answers

*"Everything you'll ever need to know is within you; the secrets of the universe are imprinted on the cells of your body."*
*~ Dan Millman*

**Time Required: Sixty Minutes**

When confronted with a drastic life change, the idea of creating a practical plan can seem ridiculous or downright impossible. After all, there is panicking to attend to, who has time to create a practical plan? You do. And you must. If you don't create a practical plan to hoist yourself out of hot water, who will?

Luckily, magick can also help you with the practical. The following recipe is a simple combination of a number of other magickal rituals.

## Ingredients

- A bright yellow candle (with no orange or red overtones)
- Paper or wooden matches
- A pen and paper to record your results
- The patience to wait on the magick to help you create a practical plan to get you out of hot water, bit by bit

## Recipe Directions

1. Give you and your Spirit Guides a spiritual boost by charging a Sun Candle (this is a mini candle spell). Get a bright yellow candle (no orange overtones), preferably in glass for safety. Sit in the South facing North with your candle in front of you. Use your paper or wooden matches to light your candle. When the flame becomes tall and strong, cup your hands around the flame, and then say in a voice of command:

*"Child of Wonder*
*Child of Flame*
*Nourish My Spirit and*
*Protect My Aim."*

2. Now set the candle to the side, send up a short prayer of thanks and request for help to the higher (if you like), and pick up your pen and paper. Think about your current life "problem or situation" and spend no more than five minutes writing a list of practical action steps that might improve your life situation. Write anything and everything that comes to mind, whether or not the idea seems useful, practical, distasteful, or impossible. Simply write. Don't think. Allow ideas to flow through the pen from higher beings onto paper. Consider your writing channeling rather than thinking. Allow the higher beings you invited into your sacred space with the Sun Candle and your request for help to flow their creativity and ideas through your pen and onto the paper.

3. Once you have completed your writing, you will now dowse your list to determine which items are meant for present use, which ideas will come in handy later, and which items you may never use. To begin, start with your non-dominant hand. Touch the tip of the index finger and thumb of that hand together so the fingers form an "O". Ensure that the other fingers are pointing slightly up so that they don't interfere with the space inside the "O" shape. Now put the index finger of your dominant hand in the center of the "O" formed by the fingers of your non-dominant hand. Say in a voice of command, "Show me Yes!" Then with force use the index finger of your dominant hand to try to break the bond of the fingers forming the "O" shape. If you are successful, then each time you are able to break the bond of the fingers forming the "O", the answer to the question you ask during dowsing is "Yes." Now repeat procedure this time saying, "Show me No!" The opposite action should occur. If the fingers parted for "Yes," they should hold together for "No." Practice this a few times so you are clear about the signals for "Yes" and "No."

4. Don't worry if you get conflicting signals at first. Simply practice the "Yes" and "No" a few times and use the most common results for "Yes" and "No." For instance, if the fingers part most of the time for "Yes," then this becomes your signal for the answer "Yes," and closed finger means "No." Don't spend a lot of time worrying about this step. Just get a feeling for the signal for each answer, and then move on to the next step.

5. In this step you will combine the list you wrote with finger-testing. For each item on the list, ask the following questions:
   - "Is this item likely to be useful in solving my life situation [describe your life situation in a few words] at all in the future?"

- "Will this item be useful in solving my life situation [describe it using the same words] either in the present or in the near future, [state a time from such as "three to six months from today"]?"
- "Will this item be useful in solving my life situation [describe it using the same words] in the far future, [state a logical time frame such as "six more months from today"]?"

6. Jot down the Yes/No answers for all three questions for each action item or possible solution you listed.

7. Rewrite your list into three separate lists, separated by whether the item on your list will be helpful in the present or near future, helpful in the far future, or not helpful at all. Don't throw away the list of items that are ostensibly "not helpful at all" because the future is always changing. A decision or action you take now or in a few weeks could move an item from one list to another.

8. Now place just the list of items that your dowsing deemed useful for the present and near future. Using the same finger-testing method, ask yourself:
   - "Are there other ideas or solutions that would be helpful to me now or in the [state your time frame for "near future" here] that are not yet on this list?"
   - If the answer is "Yes," then ask an angel to help you complete your list. Say aloud or internally,

*"I would like to request the help of an angel of Sun Yellow, Water Blue, Grass Green, and Sky Blue who specializes in [state the problem for which you want the angel's help]..."*

   - pause for a few seconds to allow the angel to appear...
   - Say aloud or internally:

*"Angel of Sun Yellow, Water Blue, Grass Green, and Sky Blue who specializes in [state the problem for which you want the angel's help], I would like to request your help in completing this list of items that will help me in the present and near future so that I can move forward in my life and solve this particular problem. I thank you in advance for your help!"*

9. Always thank higher beings in advance for their help. It is a show of good faith and is also a polite way to interact with higher beings. Then be prepared with pen and paper handy because there is a good chance that the angel will flood you with information, ideas, strategies, tactics, and insights that will amaze you! Once the flow of information has stopped, thank the angel again for the help--again, appreciation is valuable and much loved by higher beings, not to mention the only form of payment they require.

10. Now take your newly expanded list of ideas and actions that can help you tackle your sticky life problem in the present and near future. Arrange the list chronologically based on importance and timing. You can put some items concurrently if you feel that working on both items in parallel will help. Finally, if you want to double check your list, use finger testing to ask whether each item is in the correct order. If not, use finger testing to check whether the item should be moved up or down the list, and how far. How to Use the Results of Your Recipe

Once complete, you now have an plan of action for moving through, around, over, under, or simply beyond the curve ball that life has thrown at you. You no longer need to feel stuck, helpless, hopeless, or angry about your life. Take comfort in the fact that even though your hands did the writing and finger testing, angels and higher beings were guiding your pen and your fingers every step of the way.

One final piece of advice to keep in mind is the magickal principle that states, "A small change in the present produces a larger change in the future." That means that acting on even one of the seemingly insignificant items on your list could result in a much bigger change in your future. The future is never fixed but is always dependent on the present. The moral of the story is to check your "present" and "future" and "never" lists frequently to see if items need to be added, removed, shifted in position, or moved to a different list. Your fingers will always steer you in the right magickal direction!

# *Pick A Card, Any Card*

*"The universe buries strange jewels deep within us all, and then stands back to see if we can find them."*
*~ Elizabeth Gilbert*

**Time Required: Fifteen Minutes**

If you find yourself in need of magickal answers but do not have access to any magickal tools (such as a scrying bowl, Sun Candle, or a pendulum), don't worry! The Universe is more than happy to use a deck of cards to provide you with the magickal answers you see. You just need to reach out to the Universe with your question, and then choose a card to discover the Universe's magickal answer.

## Ingredients
- A quiet place to sit and formulate your question to the Universe

65

- An open mind, ready to receive magickal answers from multiple possible sources around you
- A deck of cards such as "Medicine Cards (by Jamie Sams and David Carson), Tarot Cards, Angel Cards, or any other deck of cards that attracts your attention.

## Recipe Directions

1. Find a quiet place to sit, and take a few cleansing breaths.

2. Once you are calm, ask your question to the Universe, either out loud or in your mind.

3. Pick up your deck of choice and shuffle the deck until the mix feels "right" to you.

4. Fan out the cards on a table and choose a card, or cut the deck and take the top card. Or use any method you like. Just remain consistent in your approach.

5. Most magickal or mystical card decks come with books that explain the meaning of each card, often with each card having two different meanings depending on whether the card is upright or reversed. Once you have chosen your card, note its position (upright or reversed) and then read the meaning of the card in the accompanying book. This card will provide the answer to your question.

## How to Use the Results of Your Recipe

Most of the time the information related to the card will mesh neatly with your question. If the meaning of the card does not seem to provide the answers you seek, hold the meaning of the card in mind as you go about your day. Chances are that the meaning of the card will appear more clearly as the day goes on. Pay attention to your interactions with others, your internal thoughts and patterns, and the situations you encounter. This simple ritual done daily helps you to operate from a place of consciousness rather than from mechanical reactions and habits, builds your relationship with the Universe, and actively brings magic into your life. If you do not receive your answer during the day, sleep on it, and see what your dreams tell you about the card. Answers may trickle through your mind and consciousness in the most amusing and interesting ways.

[this page intentionally left blank]

# *More Magickal Resources*

## Kindle or Paperback on Amazon:
1. *Witchcraft Spell Book Series:*
   - Learn How to Do Witchcraft Rituals and Spells with Your Bare Hands (Witchcraft Spell Books, Book 1)
   - Learn How to Do Witchcraft Rituals and Spells with Household Ingredients (Witchcraft Spell Books, Book 2)
   - Learn How to Do Witchcraft Rituals and Spells with Magical Tools (Witchcraft Spell Books, Book 3)
   - Witchcraft Spell Book: The Complete Guide of Witchcraft Rituals & Spells for Beginners (compilation of Books 1, 2 & 3)
2. *Kitchen Table Magick Series*

## Ebooks and Online Courses at www.shamanschool.com
- Wand: Air Tool
- Athame: Fire Tool
- Chalice: Water Tool
- Plate: Earth Tool
- Magical Tool: Firebowl
- Psychic Development
- Energy Healing For Self and Others

- How to Do Voodoo
- Daily Rituals to Attract What You Want in Life

***Find a complete list of magickal resources on https://amzn.to/3swxvPo. These resources are constantly updated so check back often!***

# Free Gift Offer

To thank you for purchasing this book, I'd like to give you a

100% FREE GIFT

Learn more about your free magickal gift.

## *Access Your Free Gift at*
## *www.shamanschool.com*

*Find a complete list of magickal resources on*
*https://amzn.to/3swxvP0. These resources are*
*constantly updated so check back often!*

# About G. Alan Joel

Magick means many things to different people. The form of magick taught by G. Alan Joel for more than 30 years is steeped in tribal traditions from around the world, from both modern tribal cultures and those from the past, which have been mostly passed on through oral dialog.

At the very heart of the magick that Mr. Joel teaches is the use of Universal Laws for the benefit of self, others, and even the planet. These magickal traditions can take on many forms, including simple rituals for daily use, specific spells for particular life situations, the use of simulacra (often better known as voodoo), weather working, water witching, the use of the elemental tools (Firebowl, Wand, Athame, Chalice, and Plate), magickal self-defense rituals, and more. Also included are the use of the Tarot for divination and spellwork, divination rituals of all kinds, Spirit-to-Spirit communication, exercises for psychic development, and abundant healing techniques.

Through his 30 plus years of studying, teaching, and honing his magickal practice, G. Alan Joel has helped thousands of people successfully integrate the magickal, and seemingly miraculous, into their daily lives. In fact, one of the greatest gifts Mr. Joel has offered through his teachings is the ability for his students to always find a magickal solution for life situations that often seem impossible to solve. With magick, anything is possible in the mundane world. All that is required of the practitioner is an open mind, the desire to learn, and a willingness to pay some time and effort into his or her magickal practice. One of Mr. Joel's favorite quotes is:

*"What you pay into your practice pays you back!"*

While many magickal traditions have fiercely guarded their secrets from the public, Mr. Joel feels that "Magick is the birthright of every planetary citizen." As such he strives to offer magickal teachings that are easily learned and inexpensive (no excessive fees to join exclusive magickal groups or ascend up the levels of learning). He also offers techniques that are usable and effective for all who are sincere in their desire to practice magick. In essence, Mr. Joel's methods teach a form of "Every Man's (and Woman's) Magick." All are welcome, his teachings are simple yet effective, and he also offers online classes in which he helps students troubleshoot their magickal issues in an interactive setting.

Find out more about Mr. Joel's teachings here and on his website (**_www.shamanschool.com_**) where magickal offerings are updated on a regular basis.

Mr. Joel augments this magickal knowledge and teaching with 30 years of practice as Doctor of Chinese Medicine, including a deep understanding of herbology and acupuncture. His understanding of the healing arts deepens the magickal knowledge he teaches, as magickal healing is a major aspect of his teachings. Mr. Joel believes that while there is clearly a time and place for Western Medicine, magickal and Eastern healing techniques can be harmoniously blended in to offer people many choices for healing all types of health conditions.

## *About the Esoteric School of Shamanism and Magic*

The Esoteric School of Shamanism and Magic was started from a desire for all people from all over the globe to be able to attend a real, if virtual, school dedicated to magick and shamanism. The aim of the Esoteric School of Shamanism and Magic is to help people create permanent, positive change in their lives through the study of esoteric magickal and shamanic knowledge. It doesn't matter what your esoteric background is, whether you started out with witchcraft, religious studies, spirituality or candle magick, we welcome you. We believe that the Truth is the same, no matter which form you practice. We delight in all manner of shamanic schools and traditions, magickal techniques and esoteric ritual. You can visit us at ***www.shamanschool.com***, our blog at ***http://shamanmagic.blogspot.com***, or on social media via links on our website.

[this page intentionally left blank]

[this page intentionally left blank]

[this page intentionally left blank]

[this page intentionally left blank]

www.ingramcontent.com/pod-product-compliance
Lightning Source LLC
Chambersburg PA
CBHW070547030426
42337CB00016B/2386